Designer Dogs

Schnoodles

by Ruth Owen

PowerKiDS press

New York

Published in 2013 by The Rosen Publishing Group, Inc.
29 East 21st Street, New York, NY 10010

First Edition

Produced for Rosen by Ruby Tuesday Books Ltd
Editor for Ruby Tuesday Books Ltd: Mark J. Sachner
US Editor: Sara Antill
Designer: Emma Randall

Photo Credits:
Cover, 1, 3, 4–5, 7, 8–9, 10–11, 12–13, 14–15, 17, 18–19, 20, 22, 25, 30 © Shutterstock; 21 © Tony Campbell; 23 © Valerie Thompson; 26–27 © Istock; 28–29 © Judy Brown.

Library of Congress Cataloging-in-Publication Data

Owen, Ruth, 1967–
 Schnoodles / by Ruth Owen. — 1st ed.
    p. cm. — (Designer dogs)
 Includes index.
 ISBN 978-1-4488-7859-8 (library binding) — ISBN 978-1-4488-7912-0 (pbk.)
 — ISBN 978-1-4488-7918-2 (6-pack)
 1. Schnoodle—Juvenile literature. I. Title.
 SF429.S378O94 2013
 636.72—dc23
                                    2012001535

Manufactured in the United States of America

CPSIA Compliance Information: Batch #B1S12PK: For Further Information contact Rosen Publishing, New York, New York at 1-800-237-9932

Contents

Meet a Schnoodle

What is super smart and super cute, and has curly hair and whiskers? It's a schnoodle!

Schnoodles are a **crossbreed** dog. This means they are a mixture of two different dog **breeds**, or types. When a schnauzer and a poodle have puppies together, they make schnoodles!

Schnoodles love to be around people, and they are devoted to their owners and human families.

Adult schnauzer

Adult poodle

Schnoodle puppy

4

An adult schnoodle

Whiskers

Some schnoodles work as therapy dogs. They visit hospitals to give love and comfort to people who are sick.

5

No Sneezing with a Schnoodle

Millions of people would love to own a pet dog, but they have an **allergy** to dogs.

One of the problems is that dogs shed, or drop, lots of hair that carries tiny bits of dead skin called dander. Dog hair and dander can make allergic people sneeze or struggle to breathe.

Schnauzers and poodles have hair that does not fall out or make allergic people ill. So dog breeders mixed the two breeds. They created schnoodles, cute-looking dogs that won't make people sneeze!

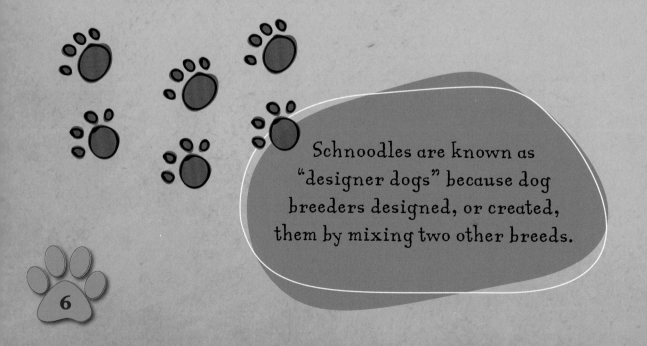

Schnoodles are known as "designer dogs" because dog breeders designed, or created, them by mixing two other breeds.

A schnoodle

Meet the Parents: Schnauzers

Schnauzers have an outer coat of rough, wiry hairs and a soft undercoat. Their hair can be all black or black and white. The black and white combo is known as "salt and pepper." Miniature schnauzers are sometimes silver and black, too.

Schnauzers come in three different sizes—miniature, standard, and giant.

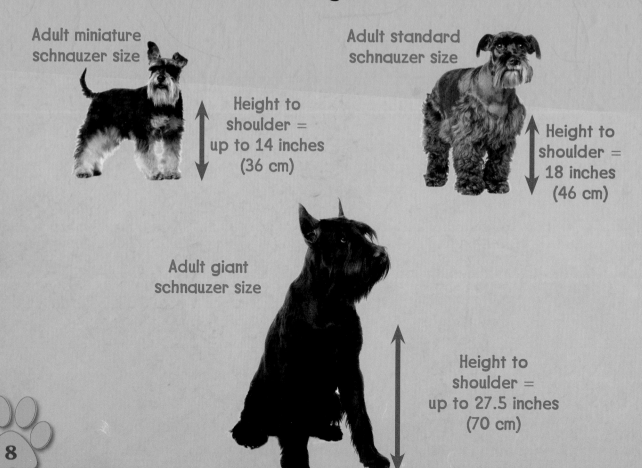

Adult miniature schnauzer size

Height to shoulder = up to 14 inches (36 cm)

Adult standard schnauzer size

Height to shoulder = 18 inches (46 cm)

Adult giant schnauzer size

Height to shoulder = up to 27.5 inches (70 cm)

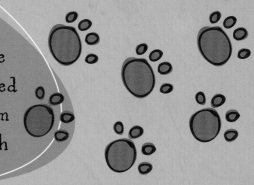

Schnauzers look as if they have a beard and mustache on their muzzles! They were first bred in Germany and get their name from the German word "schnauze," which means "snout."

A giant schnauzer

Meet the Parents: Working Schnauzers

Schnauzers were first bred hundreds of years ago to be working dogs on farms. They guarded the animals and the farmer's family. When a farmer took goods to the market, the dog guarded the family's cart while the farmer did business or took a rest.

Miniature and giant schnauzers were bred from the standard breed. The miniature dogs kept farm buildings clear of rats.

Giant schnauzers worked as guard dogs and helped farmers drive sheep. They were also trained to be police dogs!

Schnauzer owners in Germany often call their smart, fearless schnauzers "the dogs with the human brain."

Meet the Parents: Poodles

Just like schnauzers, poodles come in different sizes. The three main sizes are **toy**, miniature, and the largest, the standard poodle. There are also "tiny toy" poodles that weigh just 4 pounds (1.8 kg), and teacup poodles that weigh just 2 pounds (900 g)!

A poodle's sneeze-free coat can be black, white, apricot, red, silver, or gray. The hair may be curly or corded, like dreadlocks!

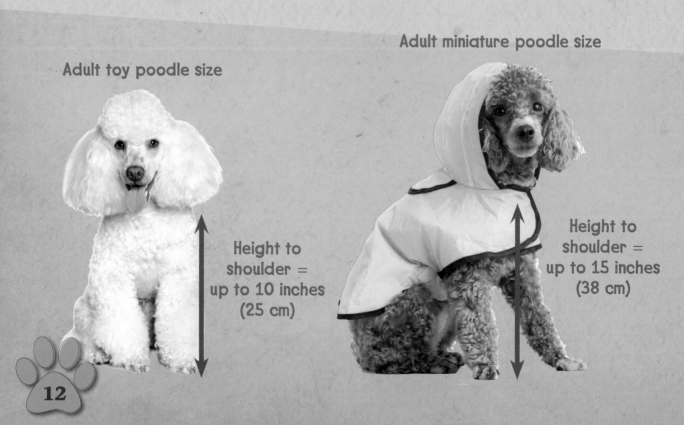

Adult miniature poodle size

Adult toy poodle size

Height to shoulder = up to 10 inches (25 cm)

Height to shoulder = up to 15 inches (38 cm)

Adult standard poodle size

A corded coat

Height to
shoulder =
over 15 inches
(38 cm)

Poodles bond
quickly with their owners and
love getting attention.
These smart dogs enjoy being
taught new things and showing
off their tricks.

13

Meet the Parents: Poodle History

Poodles were originally bred to work alongside people hunting ducks and other water birds. Once a bird had been shot, the poodle dove into the water to retrieve the bird and carry it back to its master.

Poodles love water and are very good swimmers. In fact, their name comes from the German word "pudel." It means "splashing in water."

It's fun to play fetch in the pool!

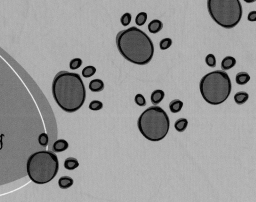

Poodles are so popular in France that people think of them as the national dog of France!

Poodles love to be at the pool.

Oodles of Personality

A schnoodle's personality is usually a mixture of all the best parts of its parents' personalities. Like its poodle parent, it will be easy to train because it will want to please its owner.

Schnoodles are also very loyal to their human families and want to stick close to them. They get this part of their personality from their schnauzer parent. Schnauzers make good guard dogs and are naturally protective of their owners.

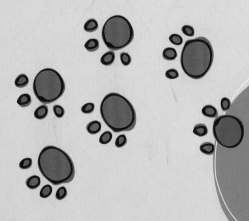

Schnoodles want to be around people and don't like being left home alone. A bored, lonely schnoodle may bark and bark, or tear up the furniture!

Schnoodle Looks

A schnoodle may look more like one of its parents than the other, or it may be a mix of both! That's the great thing about crossbreeds. Each puppy is a little different!

A schnoodle may have rough, wiry hair like a schnauzer, or soft, woolly, poodle-like hair. They can be apricot, white, gray, black, or black with white patches. They may also be a mixture of black and brown, which is known as phantom coloring.

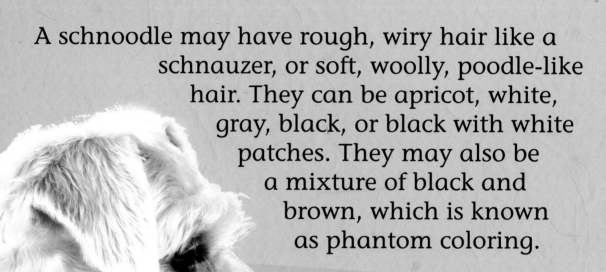

This white schnoodle has had its coat clipped, or cut.

Schnoodles don't shed their hair, so it's important to brush them every week to keep their coat tangle free. They also need a doggie haircut about four times a year.

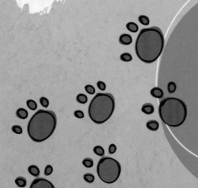

18

Mini Schnoodles, Giant Schnoodles

Like their parent breeds, schnoodles can come in many sizes.

If a standard poodle and a giant schnauzer **mate**, they will make giant schnoodles! As adults, these dogs can weigh 80 pounds (36 kg), or more. They measure up to 27 inches (69 cm) from the ground to their shoulders.

If a toy poodle and a miniature schnauzer mate, they will have toy schnoodle puppies.

Adult toy schnoodle size

Height to shoulder = up to 10 inches (25 cm)

Giant schnoodles have lots of energy and need an hour of exercise every day. They love to play in water and snow!

A giant schnoodle

Schnoodle Puppies

A schnoodle puppy may have a poodle mother and schnauzer father, or the other way around.

The mother usually gives birth to a **litter** of between two and four puppies. The little puppies drink milk from their mother.

For the first two weeks, the puppies sleep a lot. By the time they are four weeks old, they are running around, playing, and exploring.

The puppies within a single litter may be different colors. Some may look more like schnauzers, while others look like poodles.

A two-week-old schnoodle puppy

Puppy Mills

A schnoodle puppy can cost hundreds of dollars. Sadly, some people are setting up "puppy mills" to make quick money. They don't care whether the puppies they breed and sell are happy or healthy.

At a puppy mill, the dogs are kept in cages in barns. They are fed poor-quality food and may not get the medical treatment they need.

When the puppies are eight weeks old, they are shipped off to pet stores. The puppies' new owners don't realize they may be taking home a sick or unhealthy pup!

A puppy that has been raised in a cage in a barn won't be used to people and may be scared of them.

A schnoodle puppy

Happy Schnoodle Puppies

Thankfully, there are lots of caring **dog breeders** raising schnoodle puppies.

Good breeders raise their puppies in their homes. The little pups get to cuddle and play with people. They learn to trust and enjoy being around people.

The puppies are fed good-quality puppy food. They visit the vet to be checked for any health problems. New owners can visit the breeder's home to meet the puppies and the parent dogs.

Good breeders
may have a list of people waiting for a
puppy. If people are happy to go on a
waiting list, it shows they are serious
about owning a dog and are not
making a quick decision.

woof

27

Reggie the Therapy Schnoodle

Reggie the giant schnoodle works as a therapy dog. With his owner, Judy, he visits hospitals, nursing homes, and places where people with disabilities live.

Reggie and his best dog friend, Blue

When Reggie visits someone, Judy gives him the command "visit." Reggie gently puts his head into the person's lap. His new friend gets to pet him and talk to him. People who are unwell or unhappy are often smiling and feeling better after a visit from Reggie.

Sometimes Reggie will visit a person who is unable to speak. Gentle giant Reggie doesn't need words to make friends and show love.

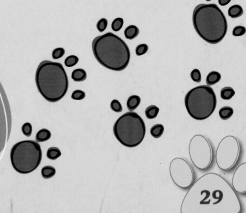

Reggie at work with
Judy (right)

Reggie plays
catch and does other tricks to help
cheer people up. At the end of a visit,
he gives a bow and a goodbye
paw wave!

Glossary

allergy (A-lur-jee) When a person's body reacts badly to something such as an animal or type of food. An allergy may make a person sneeze, get sore skin, vomit, or become seriously ill.

bond (BOND) To form a close connection based on love and trust.

breed (BREED) A type of dog. Also, the word used to describe the act of mating two dogs in order for them to have puppies.

crossbreed (KROS-breed) A type of dog created from two different breeds.

dog breeder (DAWG BREED-er) A person who breeds dogs and sells them.

litter (LIH-ter) A group of baby animals all born to the same mother at the same time.

mate (MAYT) When a male and a female animal come together to produce young.

toy (TOY) The word used to describe the size of a dog that is very small.

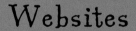

Websites

Due to the changing nature of Internet links, PowerKids Press has developed an online list of websites related to the subject of this book. This site is updated regularly. Please use this link to access the list:

www.powerkidslinks.com/ddog/schnoo/

Read More

George, Charles, and Linda George. *Miniature Schnauzer*. Top Dogs. New York: Scholastic, 2010.

MacAulay, Kelley, and Bobbie Kalman. *Poodles*. Pet Care. New York: Crabtree Publishing, 2007.

Wheeler, Jill C. *Schnoodles*. Minneapolis, MN: Checkerboard Books, 2008.

Index